# TURN A BLIND EYE

## The Nexus of corporate practice and Americans safety

By Elite
Publication

# TABLE OF CONTENTS

# Corruption and Collusion

## Interactive Exercises for each chapter

# Preface

Americans' safety is significantly impacted by the complex web of corporate operations in today's globalized society. Corporations are essential for fostering innovation and economic success , but they can also create covert risk that endanger people and communities' safety. Corporations can have a significant impact on public safety through their decisions about everything from the manufacture of commodities to the defense of intellectual property.

The goal of this handbook, "Turn a blind eye: The Nexus of Corporate Practices and Americans Safety," is to shed light on the hazards that are frequently disregarded but are a part of business operations. By examining particular instances when corporate conduct collides with public safety issues, we want to increase consciousness, promote comprehension, and motivate action to reduce these hazards. By delving deeply into important subjects and providing practical illustrations, we will expose the covert dangers presented by business practices and the pressing need for responsibility and change. Recognizing the complexity of the challenges at hand and our collective duty to ensure public safety is crucial as we set out on this path. By raising awareness of these lurking dangers and promoting accountability, openness, and moral behavior in business dealings, we may endeavor to create more secure and resilient communities for everybody.

# Chapter 1
## The China Threat

China has become a major power in the global economy as a result of its tremendous economic ascension in recent decades, which has changed the global landscape. China's ascent has brought attention to hidden risks to global public safety, nevertheless, in addition to its economic expansion. Concerns about product safety, cyber espionage, and intellectual property theft are just a few of the many issues that fall under the umbrella of the China menace, which affects people, businesses, and government systems globally.

The China Danger's History: Under Deng Xiaoping's direction, China started an economic reform and opening-up program in the late 20th century, which is when the danger originated. China's economy witnessed a shift during this time from being centrally planned to being market-oriented, which resulted in unheard-of levels of industrial and economic growth. But as China's economy grew, worries about the caliber and security of its goods also grew.

Several product safety problems involving Chinese-manufactured items surfaced in the early 2000s, making it one of the first and most visible manifestations of the China danger.

These crises, which included tainted pharmaceuticals, poisoned food, and toys, brought to light weaknesses in China's regulatory supervision and quality control systems. In addition to putting consumers at immediate risk, the mass distribution of these dangerous products also prompted concerns about the honesty of China's production processes. As China consolidated its position on the international scene, worries regarding its involvement in intellectual property theft and cyber espionage grew. Lawmakers and business executives became alarmed upon learning of reports of state-sponsored cyberattacks and corporate espionage aimed at international corporations and government organizations. Tensions between China and its trading partners were exacerbated by claims that China was involved in the theft of unique technology, trade secrets, and sensitive intellectual property. The China menace is still a major concern today, having a big impact on economic stability, national security, and public safety. Efforts to mitigate the risks associated with global trade and economic integration and address the hidden threats posed by China must rise in tandem with the country's increasing power.

# Examples & Case Studies

1. The 2008 melamine-tainted milk scandal highlighted structural flaws in

China's dairy industry and claimed the lives of newborns.

2. Chinese state-sponsored hackers were implicated in allegations of cyber espionage directed toward corporations and U.S. government agencies.

3. high-profile instances of Chinese actors stealing intellectual property, including trade secrets taken from businesses in the technology, aerospace, and pharmaceutical industries.

# Keynotes

1 The national security of the United States is seriously threatened by China's growing economic might.

2. American citizens' health and safety are at risk due to the Chinese government's contempt for safety regulations and oversight.

3. China can take advantage of American weaknesses for financial gain due to corruption and collaboration among influential persons.

4. The necessity of being more vigilant and aware of the growing threat that China's aggressive methods pose.

# Self Reflection Questions

1. In what ways has reading about China's policies changed your understanding of both national security and international economics?

_______________________________

_______________________________

_______________________________

_______________________________

_______________________________

_______________________________

_______________________________

_______________________________

_______________________________

2. Consider the times in your own life when you might have unintentionally helped Chinese companies or goods. How will this information affect the way you make purchases in the future?

3. Think about the moral ramifications of ignoring China's destructive practices. How can people and organizations assume accountability for advancing moral business conduct?

---

---

---

---

---

---

---

---

---

4. What is your opinion of the government's and regulatory bodies' involvement in countering the China threat? What modifications to regulations and oversight would you support?

# Action Plan

1. Do some research and make a list of businesses that are known to do unethical business with China. Decide

to promote ethical substitutes and boycott their products.

2. Keep up with news and developments about China's influence on the safety and security of the United States. Consider joining advocacy groups that are centered on this problem and keeping up with reputable news sources.

3. Have a conversation on the significance of making businesses and public leaders responsible for their activities toward China with friends, family, and neighbors.

4. You should write to your legislators in Congress to voice your worries about China's destructive policies and to request that they take appropriate action.

# Personal insight

# Chapter 2
## Contaminated drugs

The spread of contaminated pharmaceuticals poses a serious risk to public safety and jeopardizes people's health and well-being all over the world. The existence of contaminants in pharmaceutical products presents significant dangers to patients, healthcare systems, and public health initiatives, ranging from inadequate manufacturing methods to intentional adulteration. This chapter examines the hidden risks associated with tainted medications, illuminating the underlying causes, repercussions, and implications for international health and security.

History of Contaminated Pharmaceuticals: Incidents involving contaminated pharmaceuticals date back centuries, making it a persistent and alarming problem. However, in the present period, factors including globalization, outsourcing of drug manufacture, and inadequate regulatory supervision have made the presence of tainted drugs more noticeable. Thalidomide, a medication provided to pregnant women to treat morning sickness, was widely distributed in the mid-20th century, and this is one of the first and most prominent instances of tainted pharmaceuticals. Sadly, it was eventually discovered that thalidomide caused serious birth abnormalities in infants, sparking a worldwide health emergency and tightening laws governing medication safety and testing. The problem of tainted pharmaceuticals has not gone away in recent decades, as evidenced by the many occurrences that have brought attention to the continuous difficulties in guaranteeing the safety and caliber of pharmaceutical products. Public health is still seriously threatened by the risks connected with tainted drugs, which range from the intentional adulteration of drugs with dangerous compounds to the discovery of harmful contaminants in generic prescriptions. The production and distribution of pharmaceuticals across numerous nations with disparate regulatory requirements has raised concerns over the integrity of the pharmaceutical supply chain, namely as a result of the globalization of drug manufacture.

# Examples & Case Studies

1. The identification of potentially cancer-causing contaminants in angiotensin II receptor blocker (ARB) drugs, which prompted extensive recalls and patient safety notifications.
2. The oversulfated chondroitin sulfate contamination of heparin, a common blood thinner, which caused severe allergic responses and patient deaths.
3. There have been cases of fake drugs getting into the pharmaceutical supply chain and endangering patients by

giving them dangerous or useless prescriptions.

# Keynotes

1. Due to China's loose regulatory requirements, tainted and counterfeit medications that pose a risk to public health can be produced.

2. The entry of these medications into the American market exposes the weaknesses in the global supply chain for pharmaceuticals.

3. Profit-driven goals frequently trump safety and quality control procedures, resulting in extensive damage and fatalities.

4. The requirement for more stringent laws, checks, and balances to guarantee the integrity and safety of pharmaceuticals.

# Self Reflection Questions

1. How has the discovery of tainted Chinese pharmaceuticals affected your faith in the medical community and government oversight bodies?

_______________________________

_______________________________


2. Consider your medical procedures
and the drugs you take at the moment.
Do you know where these medications
come from and what standards are
followed throughout production?


_______________________________

_______________________________

_______________________________

_______________________________

_______________________________

_______________________________

_______________________________

_______________________________

3. Take into account the moral conundrum that Chinese pharmaceutical businesses are facing. How can these businesses reconcile their need for profit with their moral obligations to customers?

_______________________________________

_______________________________________


4. How can people fight for increased
accountability and transparency in the
pharmaceutical sector to stop the
spread of tainted medications?


_______________________________________

_______________________________________

_______________________________________

_______________________________________

_______________________________________

_______________________________________

_______________________________________

# Action Plan

1. Examine the drugs you now use and find out where they are made. Talk to your healthcare practitioner about other solutions that have been proven to meet safety criteria.

2. Learn about the dangers of tainted and counterfeit medications, especially those coming from China. To increase awareness, provide friends and family with this information.

3. Back policies and programs that attempt to improve national and international regulatory control over pharmaceutical manufacturing methods.

4. Look into ways to assist groups and projects that aim to battle fake drugs and improve drug safety, such as philanthropic contributions and advocacy campaigns.

# Personal insight

______________________________

______________________________

______________________________

______________________________

______________________________

______________________________

______________________________

______________________________

# Chapter 3

# intellectual property theft

An Introduction to Intellectual Property Theft: Theft of intellectual property (IP) is a danger to global security, economic progress, and creativity. The illegal appropriation of intellectual property compromises the integrity of markets, stifles competition, and jeopardizes the rights of creators and inventors. Examples include counterfeiting, piracy, corporate espionage, and trade secret theft. This chapter delves into the hidden risks associated with intellectual property theft, illuminating its frequency, effects, and global ramifications for economies, societies, and industries.

Intellectual Property History Theft: The idea of intellectual property has a long history, just like the theft of intellectual property. Over the ages, people and institutions have used a variety of theft and misappropriation techniques to try and make money from the concepts, innovations, and artistic creations of others. But in the present day, globalization and technological breakthroughs have made it easier for stolen trade secrets, counterfeit items, and pirated commodities to proliferate globally.

When copyrighted inventions and manufacturing methods were copied without permission during the Industrial Revolution, it became one of the first instances of intellectual property theft. Intellectual property rules and enforcement procedures emerged as a result of the increasing prevalence of infringement and piracy cases in sectors that depended more and more on intellectual property rights to safeguard their innovations.

The emergence of digital technology in recent decades has completely changed the nature of intellectual property theft, facilitating piracy, counterfeiting, and unlawful access to confidential information for both individuals and companies. The criminal trade of counterfeit goods, pirated content, and stolen intellectual property has flourished due to the growth of online markets, file-sharing platforms, and digital communication channels.

# Examples & Case Studies

1. The fashion sector has witnessed a surge in the sales of fake items, such as imitation designer handbags, apparel, and accessories, which has negatively impacted the reputation of authentic brands and caused financial losses.

2. Incidents of corporate espionage and trade secret theft affect businesses in the technology, pharmaceutical, and defense sectors and cause them to lose their competitive edge and valuable data.

3. The effects of digital piracy on the publishing, music, and film industries,

which result in lost profits, employment losses, and the degradation of intellectual property rights.

# **Keynotes**

1. The systematic theft of intellectual property by China is a serious danger to national security, economic competitiveness, and American creativity.

2. China may carry on its illegal activities without facing consequences because there are no enforcement procedures or punitive measures in place.

3. Chinese companies steal intellectual property, causing huge losses for American companies, especially in the manufacturing and technology sectors.

4. The pressing need for more robust trade policies, diplomatic initiatives, and legal safeguards to stop intellectual property theft and defend US interests.

# Self Reflection Questions

1. How has knowledge of China's theft of intellectual property affected your opinion of international commerce and economic competitiveness?

____________________________

____________________________

____________________________

____________________________

____________________________

_______________________________

_______________________________

_______________________________

_______________________________

_______________________________

2. Consider the situations in which you might have unintentionally aided businesses or goods that steal intellectual property. How does this information affect the way you shop?

_______________________________

_______________________________

_______________________________

_______________________________

_______________________________

_______________________

_______________________

_______________________

_______________________

_______________________

3. Think about the moral ramifications of stealing intellectual property and how it affects creativity and innovation. How can companies and individuals maintain moral principles when dealing with China?

_______________________

_______________________

_______________________

_______________________

_______________________

_______________________

_______________________________

_______________________________

_______________________________

_______________________________

4.. How can the whole community cooperate to confront China's theft of intellectual property? What part do you think consumers, companies, and governments will play in this endeavor?

_______________________________

_______________________________

_______________________________

_______________________________

_______________________________

_______________________________

# Action Plan

1. Examine your spending patterns to find goods or services that might be connected to the theft of intellectual property. Assert a firm commitment to endorsing companies and brands that uphold intellectual property rights and possess high ethical standards.

2. Remain up to date on the latest instances of intellectual property theft and any developments pertaining to trade agreements and court cases. For

news and commentary on these subjects, subscribe to reliable sources.

3. Push for laws and programs that safeguard intellectual property rights and make China answerable for its unethical actions. This could entail signing petitions, getting in touch with elected officials, and taking part in advocacy efforts.

4. Look for ways to encourage creativity and innovation in your neighborhood, such as going to neighborhood gatherings, lending a hand to small companies, and starting conversations on innovation and intellectual property rights.

# Personal insight

# Chapter 4
## Corruption and Collusion

The integrity of economies, cultures, and institutions across the globe is persistently threatened by corruption and collaboration. Corrupt practices degrade trust, damage democracy, and inhibit growth. Examples of these acts include bribery, embezzlement, cronyism, and nepotism. These issues are made worse by collusive ties between government officials and corporations, which allow for the abuse, fraud, and exploitation of power for one's benefit. This chapter examines the covert perils of cooperation and corruption, illuminating their incidence, effects, and ramifications for public safety, accountability, and government.

History of Corruption and Collusion: Bribery, nepotism, and favoritism have existed since the dawn of human civilization, making the history of corruption and collusion as old as civilization itself. Corrupt activities have long been common in both the public and private spheres, frequently supported by powerful people looking to further their agendas at the expense of the general welfare.

The modern period has witnessed a transformation in the terrain of corruption and collusion due to the globalization of economies and the rise of corporate influence, making them more prevalent and intricate than ever. The boundaries between public and private interests have gotten increasingly hazy due to corporate lobbying, political contributions, regulatory capture, and revolving-door politics. This has made it possible for corrupt behaviors and conspiratorial relationships to become entrenched at all levels of government and business.

# Examples & Case Studies

1. President Richard Nixon resigned as a result of the US Watergate crisis, which exposed pervasive power abuse and corruption at the highest levels of government.

2. One of the biggest corporate fraud cases in history was the Enron scandal,

which involved executives and auditors working together to falsify financial statements and mislead investors.

3. The global network of offshore tax havens used by powerful people, businesses, and political figures to avoid paying taxes and laundering money was made public by the Panama Papers leak.

# Keynotes

1. National sovereignty and democratic ideals are threatened by China's corruption and collaboration in the manipulation of American institutions, corporations, and politicians.

2. Transparency, accountability, and intellectual freedom are threatened by Chinese money and interests

influencing American politics and academics.

3. Financial gain takes precedence over ethical considerations in the cycle of corruption and exploitation perpetuated by the complicity of individuals and businesses in both countries.

4. It is essential to enhance transparency, disclosure, and regulatory supervision in order to reduce the potential hazards linked to corruption and collusion.

# Self Reflection Questions

1. What effect does it have on your faith in political and institutional integrity to learn of corruption and

collaboration between Chinese and American entities?

________________________________________

________________________________________

________________________________________

________________________________________

________________________________________

________________________________________

________________________________________

________________________________________

________________________________________

2. Think back to times in your career or personal life when you could have seen indications of corruption or

improper influence. In what ways do these encounters contribute to your comprehension of the larger problem?

_______________________________

_______________________________

_______________________________

_______________________________

_______________________________

_______________________________

_______________________________

_______________________________

_______________________________

3. Think about the moral conundrums that people and organizations

encounter when presented with chances to pursue financial success at the expense of moral values. In such circumstances, how can people resist the need to compromise their integrity?

4. How can people make institutions, corporations, and elected officials responsible for their deeds and ties to China? What actions may be implemented in the public and commercial sectors to encourage ethical behavior and transparency?

# Action Plan

1. To spot possible conflicts of interest or undue influence, familiarize yourself with the sources of funding for academic research and political campaign contributions.

2. Encourage the work of groups and projects aimed at advancing accountability and openness in government, such as watchdog groups and campaigns to reform campaign finance.

3. Talk about the value of moral behavior and integrity in both the public and private spheres with your friends, family, and neighbors. Increase public understanding of the

dangers posed by collaboration and corruption.

4. Encourage the passage of laws and policy changes that will improve regulatory monitoring, bolster disclosure standards, and counteract foreign influence in American institutions and politics.

# Personal insight

_______________________________

_______________________________

_______________________________

_______________________________

_______________________________

_______________________________